WONDER WOMEN

FRAMES
BARNA GROUP

WONDER WOMEN

Navigating the Challenges of Motherhood,
Career, and Identity

KATE HARRIS
RE/FRAME BY ANDY CROUCH

ZONDERVAN

Wonder Women
Copyright © 2013 by Barna Group

This title is also available as a Zondervan ebook.
Visit www.zondervan.com/ebooks.

This title is also available in a Zondervan audio edition.
Visit www.zondervan.fm.

Requests for information should be addressed to:

Zondervan, *Grand Rapids, Michigan 49530*

ISBN 978-0-310-43330-9 (softcover)

All Scripture quotations, unless otherwise indicated, are taken from The Holy Bible, *New International Version*®, *NIV*®. Copyright © 1973, 1978, 1984, 2011 by Biblica, Inc.™ Used by permission. All rights reserved worldwide.

Any Internet addresses (websites, blogs, etc.) and telephone numbers in this book are offered as a resource. They are not intended in any way to be or imply an endorsement by Zondervan, nor does Zondervan vouch for the content of these sites and numbers for the life of this book.

Published in association with the literary agency of The Fedd Agency, Inc, 401 Ranch Road 620 South, Suite 350c, Austin, TX 78734.

Cover design and interior graphics: Amy Duty
Interior design: Kate Mulvaney

Printed in the United States of America

13 14 15 16 17 18 /DCI/ 18 17 16 15 14 13 12 11 10 9 8 7 6 5 4 3 2 1

CONTENTS

....

WHY YOU NEED FRAMES

These days, you probably find yourself with less time than ever.

Everything seems like it's moving at a faster pace — except your ability to keep up.

Somehow, you are weighed down with more obligations than you have ever had before.

Life feels more complicated. More complex.

If you're like most people, you probably have lots of questions about how to live a life that matters. You feel as though you have more to learn than can possibly be learned. But with smaller chunks of time and more sources of information than ever before, where can you turn for real insight and livable wisdom?

Barna Group has produced this series to examine the complicated issues of life and to help you live more meaningfully. We call it FRAMES — like a good set of eyeglasses that help you see the world more clearly ... or a work of art perfectly hung that invites you to look more closely ... or a building's skeleton, the part that is most essential to its structure.

The FRAMES Season 1 collection provides thoughtful and concise, data-driven and visually appealing insights for anyone who wants a more faith-driven and fulfilling life. In each FRAME we couple new cultural analysis from our team at Barna with an essay from leading voices in the field, providing information and ideas for you to digest in a more easily consumed number of words.

After all, it's a fast-paced world, full of words and images vying for your attention. Most of us have a number of half-read or "read someday" books on our shelves. But each FRAME aims to give you the essential information and real-life application behind one of today's most crucial trends in less than one-quarter the length of most books. These are big ideas in small books— designed so you truly can read less but know more. And the infographics and ideas in this FRAME are intended for share-ability. So read it, then find someone to "frame" with these ideas, and keep the conversation going (see "Share This Frame" on page 85).

Furthermore, each FRAME brings a distinctly Christian point of view to today's trends. In times of uncertainty, people look for guides. And we believe the Christian community is trying to make sense of the dramatic social changes happening around us.

Over the past thirty years, Barna Group has built a reputation as a trusted analyst of religion and culture. We offer cultural discernment for the Christian community by thoughtful analysts who care enough to tell the truth about what's really happening in today's society.

So sit back, but not for long. With FRAMES we invite you to read less and know more.

DAVID KINNAMAN
FRAMES, executive producer
president / Barna Group

ROXANNE STONE
FRAMES, general editor
vice president / Barna Group

Learn more at www.barnaframes.com.

FRAMES

TITLE	20 and Something	Becoming Home	Fighting for Peace	Greater Expectations
PURPOSE	Have the Time of Your Life (And Figure It All Out Too)	Adoption, Foster Care, and Mentoring – Living Out God's Heart for Orphans	Your Role in a Culture Too Comfortable with Violence	Succeed (and Stay Sane) in an On-Demand, All-Access, Always-On Age
AUTHOR	David H. Kim	Jedd Medefind	Carol Howard Merritt & Tyler Wigg-Stevenson	Claire Diaz-Ortiz
KEY TREND	27% of young adults have clear goals for the next 5 years	62% of Americans believe Christians have a responsibility to adopt	47% of adults say they're less comfortable with violence than 10 years ago	42% of people are unhappy with their work/life balance

PERFECT FOR SMALL GROUP DISCUSSION

FRAMES Season 1: DVD
FRAMES Season 1: The Complete
          Collection

READ LESS.
KNOW MORE.

The Hyperlinked Life	Multi-Careering	Sacred Roots	Schools in Crisis	Wonder Women
Live with Wisdom in an Age of Information Overload	Do Work that Matters at Every Stage of Your Journey	Why Church Still Matters	They Need Your Help (Whether You Have Kids or Not)	Navigating the Challenges of Motherhood, Career, and Identity
Jun Young & David Kinnaman	Bob Goff	Jon Tyson	Nicole Baker Fulgham	Kate Harris
71% of adults admit they're overwhelmed by information	75% of adults are looking for ways to live a more meaningful life	51% of people don't think it's important to attend church	46% of Americans say public schools are worse than 5 years ago	72% of women say they're stressed

#BarnaFrames

www.barnaframes.com

Barna Group

 ZONDERVAN®

BEFORE YOU READ

....

- When you think of what balance might look like in your life, what do you imagine?

- If there was one area of your life you could improve, what would it be?

- What does the word *vocation* mean to you?

- If you could sum up your life—your roles, passions, the many hats you wear—in one sentence, what would it be?

- Where do you feel most alive in your life? Where do you feel most drained?

- How has the church helped you make sense of your personal calling? In what ways has it supported the work you do—as a woman, wife, mother, employee, creator, and so on?

- When you think about what you *want* your life to look like, what do you picture? How is that different from the life you are living now?

WONDER WOMEN

Navigating the Challenges of Motherhood,
Career, and Identity

INFOGRAPHICS

It's COMPLICATED

Women see themselves as far from one-dimensional and
describe family, friends, career, personal interests, and faith
as all central to shaping their identity.

What Shapes You?

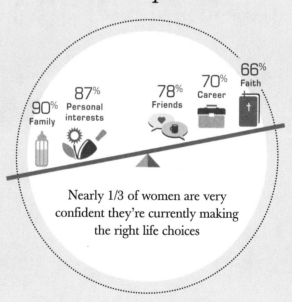

90%
Family

87%
Personal
interests

78%
Friends

70%
Career

66%
Faith

Nearly 1/3 of women are very
confident they're currently making
the right life choices

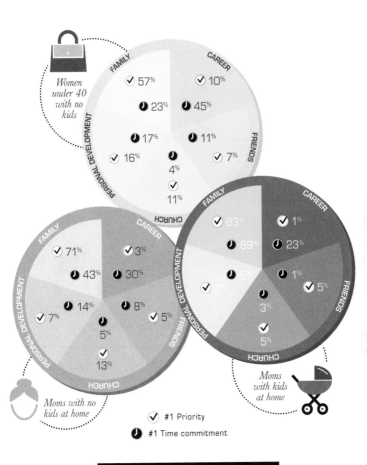

Women under 40 with no kids

	FAMILY	CAREER
#1 Priority	57%	10%
#1 Time commitment	23%	45%
#1 Time commitment	17%	11%
	PERSONAL DEVELOPMENT 16%	FRIENDS 7%
#1 Time commitment	4%	
#1 Priority CHURCH	11%	

Moms with no kids at home

	FAMILY	CAREER
#1 Priority	71%	3%
#1 Time commitment	43%	30%
	PERSONAL DEVELOPMENT 14%	FRIENDS 8%
#1 Priority	7%	5%
#1 Time commitment	5%	
#1 Priority CHURCH	13%	

Moms with kids at home

	FAMILY	CAREER
#1 Priority	83%	1%
#1 Time commitment	69%	23%
	PERSONAL DEVELOPMENT 5%	FRIENDS 1% / 5%
#1 Time commitment	3%	
#1 Priority CHURCH	5%	

✓ #1 Priority
🕐 #1 Time commitment

Priorities vs. Time

We don't always get to spend the most time on the things that are
most important to us—a source of frustration for many people.
Generally though, women are able to dedicate their time in
alignment with their priorities … except when it comes to work.

I can't get no
SATISFACTION

While three-quarters of women say they are satisfied with their life, there is a lot going on under the surface.

All women

50% Somewhat satisfied

26% Extremely satisfied

Moms*

58% Somewhat satisfied

19% Extremely satisfied

DISSATISFIED WITH WORK/ HOME BALANCE	STRESSED OUT	TIRED	OVERCOMMITTED
62% Moms	**80%** Moms	**70%** Moms	**56%** Moms
59% All women	**72%** All women	**58%** All women	**48%** All women

WANT TO DO BETTER IN AT LEAST ONE AREA OF LIFE:

 **95%** Moms

 88% All women

*Women with children still at home

I feel overcommitted ...

31% Moms

26% Moms

6% Moms

9% Moms

25% All women

18% All women

5% All women

8% All women

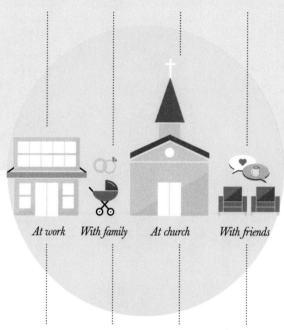

At work *With family* *At church* *With friends*

I would like to improve ...

15% Moms

12% Moms

24% Moms

15% Moms

14% All women

17% All women

22% All women

14% All women

WONDER WOMEN

Navigating the Challenges of Motherhood,
Career, and Identity

FRAMEWORK

BY BARNA GROUP

Whether to lean in or opt out, go to work or work from home, win the bread or care for the kids — even have kids or not — are the choices women in America today must make.

And they're not easy to make. For whatever you decide will affect a host of responsibilities, including your family, your faith, your career, your friends, your personal health, and your dreams for the future.

What is God's purpose for my life? That's a hard enough question. But when you add the daily realities of grocery shopping, laundry, working out, and sneaking in a Skype business call during nap time or before the latest juice spill, it's difficult to see any answer clearly.

The perceptions of others don't make this choice any easier. The ongoing "Mommy Wars," expectations of gender roles within the culture and the church, and the cultural cry of "having it all" only further complicate a woman's sense of calling and identity.

So what's a woman to do? In our FRAMES research, we surveyed women to find out exactly how they feel about their commitments to family, church, career, and community, and the tensions that pull them often in seemingly opposite directions.

One striking thing we learned is that while three-quarters of women are generally satisfied with their lives, there's also a lot going on underneath the surface.

To start with, most women in the US (59%) are dissatisfied with their personal balance between work and home life. This rate increases among women raising

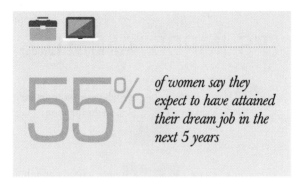

55% *of women say they expect to have attained their dream job in the next 5 years*

children (62%). Another 72% of women say they are overwhelmed by stress, and 58% say they do not get enough rest. According to Pew Research, among working moms, 40% say that whatever they are doing, they *always* feel rushed.

And yet, women in all circumstances are aspirational. They have a clear sense of how they would like to improve their lives. When asked what they want to accomplish before age thirty, younger women (18–29) hope to finish their education (53%), launch their career (50%), find out who they really are (45%), and become more spiritually mature (33%). And more than half (55%) believe that in the next five years they will have attained their dream job. The data also reveal women with children (66%) count launching their career as an important goal even more so than do childless women (50%), suggesting that moms who may have delayed professional plans for children still hope for a significant career ahead.

The question that has captured the cultural imagination

By the age of 30,
IT'S IMPORTANT TO...

Moms		Under 40, no kids

32% **27%**

Become more mature spiritually

72% **67%**

Become financially independent

31% **27%**

Enjoy life

50% **44%**

Find out who I really am

66% **52%**

Finish my education

66% **50%**

Start a career

18% **22%**

Travel abroad

today—can women have it all?—is still widely debated. Yet there can be no question about this: most women *want* it all.

The Priorities of Modern Women

How we spend our time is often a portrait of our priorities—though the reality of our time commitments doesn't always paint the portrait we wish it would.

All moms rank family as their number one priority, and they say it is also their number one time commitment. This is especially true, as you might expect, for moms with kids still at home: seven out of ten say family is their number one time commitment. What stands out, however, is the fact that no other time commitment is even a remote close second. Just over two out of ten moms say they spend most of their time every week on their career. Even fewer say they spend the most hours in a week on personal development (5%), church (3%), or friendships (1%). Where moms clearly feel the most disparity between their priorities and their time commitments is when it comes to work. While moms rank career as last on their list of priorities, it comes in second on their list of time commitments.

After family, women with kids at home prioritize personal time and development, church, friendships, and career in that order. And, aside from work, they seem mostly able to appropriately align their time commitments with those priorities.

Women under 40 without children are a slightly

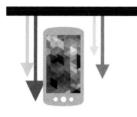

INFERIORITY COMPLEX

When comparing themselves to others via social media, practicing Christian women tend to feel that other people are "better than me" in the following ways:

11:1
Status and prestige*

10:1
Creativity

3:1
Ability to accomplish tasks

2:1
Career or job

*They are 11 times more likely to say they feel "worse than their friends" than to say they feel "better than their friends"

different story. While they still list family as their first priority (57%), they say career takes up the most time (45%). And how they prioritize beyond family follows a similar pattern to moms, except they prioritize career slightly over friendships.

One of the interesting things the research revealed was the low priority women seem to put on friendships. The research consistently shows friendship showing up near the bottom of priorities and time commitments for all women. Between career pursuits and family pressures, friends often get short shrift. And yet, more than one-third agree with the statement, "I am often lonely." This statistic is not much different among practicing Christian women—27% describe themselves as often lonely.

Of course, moms prioritizing family is to

be expected. It's also not surprising that the family is where most mothers spend the majority of their time, and that career or work rises higher on the priority list for women without children. While these facts are not particularly surprising, they are the strings that pull women apart in their demands for time, heart, and emotions, and this is where the tenuous balancing act comes in.

American women do not define themselves by any one-dimensional role, but view their personal identity in a variety of ways. Whether or not they are moms, an overwhelming 90% of women say family is central to their identity. At the same time, 66% of women say faith is central to their perception of who they are. And finally, 70% say their career informs their understanding of personal identity.

SUPERIORITY COMPLEX

Practicing Christian women tend to say that social media makes them feel that other people are "worse than me" when it comes to:

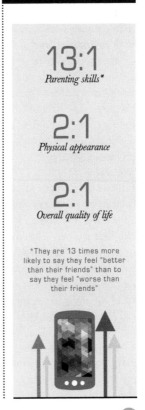

13:1
Parenting skills*

2:1
Physical appearance

2:1
Overall quality of life

*They are 13 times more likely to say they feel "better than their friends" than to say they feel "worse than their friends"

In reality no woman has 100% of herself to give to each arena of her life every day without becoming woefully overcommitted. Yet it doesn't stop many from trying — and that's where burnout often overshadows any hope for meaningful living.

Stressed Out, Dissatisfied, and Overcommitted

While moms with kids at home say they are satisfied with their family life (61%), for many it's also the greatest source of stress. For example, 42% of all women are satisfied with the amount of rest in their lives, and this number drops significantly for moms with kids at home — only 30% of whom say the same. Additionally, moms (20%) are nearly twice as likely as women without kids (12%) to become stressed to the point of physical illness.

Discontent also creeps in when moms begin to compare their lives with other women. Overall, moms with children in the house (14%) are twice as likely as childless women (7%) to view the quality of life of other women in their social circles as superior. Likewise, women with children are twice as likely to believe their female peers have a better career life (21% compared to 11%) and a better life in terms of financial comfort (22% compared to 10%).

Then there are the struggles with commitment — at work and at home. Nearly one-third of moms (31%) say they have too many commitments at work, while about one-quarter (26%) feel they are overcommitted at home. Yet in other area of life, women often feel they're not committed enough. Strikingly, the number one area American women name where they can improve is church—22% say they'd like to be more involved in a community of faith.

Half the Church

Perhaps the best way to welcome women into churches is not to saddle them upon entry with an array of "shoulds" to add to their lists of commitments. Instead, women need to find a place of support that recognizes the value of their many hats and empowers them to live well into those roles. And right now, the data suggest women are not finding such a place at church. For moms who admit they are struggling to balance work, family, and personal priorities, a startling 42% say faith communities do not offer them any emotional or social support "at all." The numbers are better among self-identified Christian women, but still, nearly half (46%) say the church only offers them "some" support and 34% admit to not receiving much or any support from their church.

Today's unique professional and cultural environments present exciting and unprecedented opportunities for women. Yet these opportunities come with questions. As society and women wrestle with the implications of varying roles for women, we will all experience some growing pains. Women will wonder what they "should" do, what they can do, what they *want* to do. And men will ask how and if their roles are changing and what it means to be the best kind of husband, father, coworker,

"Church provides emotional support for me"

Women under 40, no kids

Moms with kids under 18

Moms, no kids at home

Practicing Christian women

very much so
somewhat
not too much
not at all

and brother. They are weighty questions—both philosophical and practical—and the church, with its rich tradition and its incarnational gospel, is an institution perfectly poised to help answer these questions and to offer a sufficient framework to approach these new realities.

Kate Harris, a mother of three and the leader of an organization dedicated to vocation and calling, has been offering women and the church a holistic context within which to have these discussions through the renewal of old words like *coherence*, *constraint*, and *consent*. Kate challenges women to move beyond the cultural conversations of "having it all" and "finding balance" to gain a more holistic idea of calling and identity. And she insists the church, more than any other institution, can lead the way. ◆

WONDER WOMEN

Navigating the Challenges of Motherhood,
Career, and Identity

THE FRAME

BY KATE HARRIS

Complexity
and Confusion

Today with much more freedom to choose our own
way in the world, we are more likely to lose ourselves
in the process.

—Lilian Calles Barger, *Eve's Revenge*[1]

Several months ago a colleague and I had lunch with
a dynamic married couple who own a prominent
international gifts business. Together, they extensively
engage in various philanthropic and civic activities in
their local community and around the world. They
each put great thought and care into raising their three
school-age children. Additionally, they enjoy time with
friends, participate in the arts, and serve their church
community.

At one point during the meal, curious to hear for myself
how this bright, well-educated, capable mother of three
viewed her various roles and responsibilities, I asked
what she made of it all. Her reply has stuck with me:
"I joke that all I do is drive a minivan because it's just
too complicated to explain everything—it would
take too long."

My heart sank, even as I had the urge to lift up my
lemonade glass with a hearty "Hear, hear!" I felt a
twinge of grief because this incredibly multi-talented
woman feels there is no adequate category to make
sense of her full and complex life. At the same time,
she was articulating what most women I know feel so
acutely, regardless of whether or not they are mothers:
"I could tell you all the dimensions of my life and work

and family and efforts, but it would just take too long to explain."

This lack of language is not a crisis in itself. But it is illustrative of a much larger tension that exists in the lives of many modern women. We don't merely need better ways to express and articulate all we do in a given day. We need sufficient frameworks to make coherent sense of our lives, longings, and experiences as women.

In my own life as a mother of three children — ages two, five, and six — and director of a small organization, I am no casual observer to this tension. On the one hand, I find deep joy and satisfaction in my role and responsibilities as a wife and mother. I aspire to fully and imaginatively steward the gifts of my family and home. At the same time, I feel drawn to launch new projects, meet new people, and engage in all manner of interests and responsibilities that take me away from home.

In general, I'm comfortable with how my various responsibilities hold together to bring rich multi-dimensionality into my life and identity. But at other times, I acutely feel the disparity between my roles and responsibilities. My passions feel at odds with each other, threatening to tear my sanity and/or my soul to bits.

I know my experience is limited to my circumstance as a married woman privileged to be able to work only part-time. Yet I also know I am not alone in feeling my work and identity are fraught with unavoidable tension.

My friend Maria, for example, who works in international development and is a PhD candidate, wonders if having children is at odds with her sense of professional and ministry calling. She longs to be faithful in her life and marriage, but she finds it hard to imagine how caring for children could fit into an already full life.

Other women, like my mom, who worked for years as a single parent to support three girls, are often so occupied keeping food on the table that any prospect of "balance" seems laughable.

For women like my friend Elizabeth, a mother of two young children and a key leader of a global organization, the incessant demands of family, work, and travel mean significant trade-offs. Her schedule is often too packed to meaningfully invest in her marriage or close friends.

I know countless women like my friend Carrie, a well-established single professional in her early forties, who is fed up with being excluded from conversations about what it means to be a woman juggling complex responsibilities simply because her life is not lived in the context of marriage and motherhood.

This vague and widespread sense of unrest, confusion, and complexity among women is evident in the inconsistency with which women report their satisfaction with life. For example, when asked about their satisfaction with life, more than three-quarters of women (76%) say they are either "extremely satisfied"

(26%) or "somewhat satisfied" (50%). While slightly fewer mothers say they are "extremely satisfied" with life (19%), their overall satisfaction number is even higher, at 77%.

But even with a sense of overall satisfaction, most women see room for improvement. In fact, 88% of women and 95% of moms say they want to substantially do better in at least one area of their life, whether family relationships, personal development, friendships, work, or religious involvement.

Furthermore, burnout rates among working women show that nearly two-thirds of moms with kids at home (62%) are dissatisfied with the balance they have between their work life and home life. Eight in ten moms say they are dissatisfied with the amount of stress they experience in their life, and seven in ten do not feel they get enough rest. These numbers are slightly better among women who do not have children, yet nearly two-thirds (63%) still say their lives are too stressful.

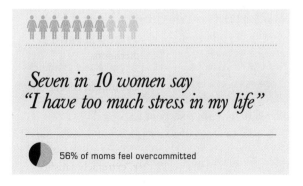

Seven in 10 women say "I have too much stress in my life"

56% of moms feel overcommitted

In short, while women claim they are generally pretty happy with their lives, they simultaneously convey significant dissatisfaction with life's basic rhythms and components.

A contradiction of this scale will have many contributing factors—including new roles and expectations for women in a rapidly changing cultural and economic landscape—but the bottom line is that the modern American woman's life is complicated.

Advancements over the past century allowing women increased access to education, a diversity of career options, flexible work arrangements, and freedom to manage fertility and childbirth are mostly welcomed as signs of progress. Most women I know don't complain about these opportunities. Yet while women report satisfaction with the general quality of life, they are profoundly unhappy with the means, pace, and cost with which they must go about attaining such opportunities. As my friend Heather, an Ivy League alumnus and mother of three, once remarked, "I don't really feel like I need more choices. I just need help knowing what to pick."

As a Christian woman seeking to navigate the fullness of my work, calling, and identity in obedience to Christ, I have been largely dissatisfied with the frameworks offered to me—by society or the church.

Culturally, there is ample commentary when it comes to this work-life balance. The "Mommy Wars," as we like to call them, have been waging for some time, and our lifestyle choices have often been caught in the crossfire. Both Ann-Marie Slaughter's *Atlantic* retrospective on "having it all"[2] and Sheryl Sandberg's counsel to "lean in,"[3] importantly name the angst that feels so palpable to modern women. But each of these frameworks also has its limits. Most of them, I find, tend to come down to better managing logistics, to finding a way to "make it work" as *Project Runway*'s Tim Gunn so famously advises.[4] But for me, while practical tips go a long way, "making it work" is only half the dilemma. Logistics alone can't bring peace or fulfillment. Women need more than that to address their deeply held tensions. Furthermore, logistical solutions depend on — or assume — a certain level of privilege and flexibility.

Likewise, when I look to the church for wisdom about the complexity of calling, motherhood, and work outside the home, I am most often encouraged to embrace the "season" of mothering young kids. Or I am drawn into a debate about gender roles in the church. The conventional church wisdom tells me the tensions I experience in scheduling, child care, travel, or finances can be assuaged if I just go easy, rest a bit, hang in there. When my kids are older I can easily move on to the next season, and perhaps that might include other work. The gender role discussion suggests my questions can be answered once and for all if I align with a particular theological camp.

And while I absolutely agree we live in time and are governed by the realities of season and circumstance (no doubt, mothering babies and young children is utterly exhausting!), I chafe at the implicit — or explicit —

suggestion that "other work" *is inevitably* for later. That it is somehow inherently separate from my work as a mother. Or even that such work is at odds with engaged and attentive mothering.

In the same way, I believe a biblical understanding of gender matters significantly in the lives of both men and women. But when my honest question about stewardship and calling is met with an abstract theological discussion about my "role," I always feel a bit put off.

These frameworks aren't inherently bad. Many of them hold significant and important grains of truth. They simply don't feel sufficient for the pressing questions in my life right now—today. None helps me, for example, in discerning whether or not to volunteer as a "room parent" in my son's classroom. On the one hand, regular involvement at his school may be good stewardship of my responsibilities as a mother. On the other hand, stepping into a role that is time intensive and falls outside my natural abilities may exhaust the time and energy I could steward more fully in other areas.

This is the kind of real-time question I need wisdom to address. The point, of course, is not whether I should be the room parent—nor is it a once-and-for-all imperative on how clean my house should be, how often I should be traveling for work, how many dinners I should be cooking weekly, how many orgasms I should be having, how often I should work out, or what size dress to wear. These parameters are far too rigid. Instead, a sufficient framework would provide principles, practices, and guidelines to help women

make more coherent, satisfying, and sustainable choices
suitable to their own unique everyday circumstances.

Vocation

Callings are complex and sometimes collide.
—Andi Ashworth, *Real Love for Real Life*[5]

In my own life, the Christian concept of vocation
has helped me think about my various longings and
responsibilities. Vocation today is often understood
in terms of a job or career, but historically it meant
much more than that. When we understand its deeper
significance, we find a meaningful and consistent
framework to help us think about our multiple life
commitments.

The root of the word *vocation* comes from the Latin
word *vox*, which means "voice." As my friend, colleague,
and author of *The Fabric of Faithfulness,* Dr. Steven
Garber says, vocation is best understood as "one's entire
life lived in response to God's voice."

Garber also clarifies the distinction between our
occupations and our vocation. An occupation is, quite
literally, that which occupies our time. So it's parenting,
writing, project managing—whatever it is we invest
our time in. But a vocation is much more broad—it
comprises all our various occupations over a lifetime.
It also accounts for our personality, our relationships,
our choices, our formation—the whole of our unique
personhood. Our occupations are always in flux,
changing in season, and they often include the little

"v" vocations or little "c" callings we sometimes use to describe our more significant roles: wife, doctor, New Yorker, mother, worship leader. In contrast, our capital "V" Vocation is a work in progress—we are ever and always living into it over the course of a lifetime. It is a winding journey to follow God's voice wherever it may lead. As Psalm 84:5 says: "Blessed are those whose strength is in [God], whose hearts are set on pilgrimage."

This definition of vocation—as a lifelong response to God's voice—is the closest I have come to finding a framework big enough to make sense of my life and work. It gives space for the dimensionality of my identity as a daughter, sister, wife, writer, friend, manager, and more. It gives account for the physical work of pregnancy and nursing, while never insisting those wearying months be wholly separate from other efforts such as writing an article during nap time, teaching my other children to read, or attending a seminar. This understanding of vocation never makes me choose once and for all between the thrill of crafting a new grant program and the simple joy of visiting with a good friend late into the evening. I can live into my vocation in both places—allowing it to inform the work I do and the kind of friend I am.

Such a definition of vocation will ask me to make practical trade-offs. But vocation never asks me to compartmentalize my life into artificial categories of "work" and "life," or "home" and "market." Vocation offers the possibility that my life and my faith can be richly and imaginatively stewarded as a whole that is far greater than the sum of its parts.

For my friend Susan, a letterpress stationery designer and mother of three children, this understanding of vocation is what helps her coherently tether what previously felt like competing interests. When her first son was still an infant, honoring the fullness of her vocation simply meant allowing time and permission to read design blogs and magazines she enjoyed. Then she decided to take a letterpress class. Soon she began to teach design classes at a nearby stationery retailer. Eventually she and her husband decided to buy a small press she could experiment with in the evenings while her husband was in business school classes. Over time, paying attention to what captured her imagination helped define the unique design aspects—like texture and packaging—that are now a signature of her style.

Like every act of faithfulness, vocation is pursued in small, gradual, ordinary ways. It is not as though Susan woke up one day and found herself owning a small-but-steadily-growing business alongside caring for three kids. Instead, because she was willing to imagine, to experiment, to believe God gave her skills and interests and passions for a purpose, her various occupations are thriving. Today, with two kids in school, she would not say she's "arrived" at her vocation. But she has a lot of clarity about work and identity from living into it over many years, responding to God's voice along the way.

My sister, Ashley, is single, works in the health-care profession, and daily battles a chronic illness. When she began to see her work as stewardship instead of striving, she was able to live more sustainably within the realities of low energy and regular medical treatments. She now works a part-time schedule that honors her physical limitations. Yet because healing is such an embedded theme in her own life and her profession, vocation has led her to become involved in the healing prayer ministry at our church and to care for elderly parishioners in our congregation. She does not yet know if marriage and children will be part of her life, but she lives in close proximity to our house in order to make the most of the family and home and kids that are near her. In countless ways she is pushing against the temptation to wait for some vague future life and instead is stewarding the life and interests already in front of her.

On the mantel over my fireplace I keep a quote by Annie Dillard, who writes, "How we spend our days, of course, is how we spend our lives."[6] For me, this is a welcome but uncomfortable reminder that, like Susan and Ashley, the life I am living today is not disconnected from the life I want to be living in the long run. It is a statement about vocation, responsibility, and stewardship. It reminds me the tenuous push and pull of my daily realities matter because this is the only day, so far as I know, I have been given by God to live. I am not guaranteed a far-off future life where all things tidily converge into bliss.

Instead, God cares that I steward the life that is in front of me right now. To wrestle and wrangle or muddle my way through it—whatever it takes—but always to insist that it makes sense, that it holds together. To believe the details of our days really do connect to some bigger purpose God has for our lives.

In her simple, straightforward way, Dillard expresses

why an inconsistency revealed in our FRAMES survey is a problem. She reminds us it is not enough to be generally satisfied with life if we are not also working hard to be satisfied with the ordinary realities of rest, stress, boundaries, and relationships that comprise our lives.

It is a deeply held truth among Christians that we are made to be whole—to live life "to the full" (John 10:10), as Jesus states, in coherence rather than fragmentation. This is exactly why it's so important for the church to understand the discrepancies between women's general satisfaction with life and their significant dissatisfaction in the gritty daily details. Our polarizing culture is limited in what it can offer women without creating more tension, criticism, and general angst. The church, on the other hand, is uniquely equipped to explore the tensions revealed in the lives of modern women. The doctrines of creation, the incarnation, and the Trinity all shed light, in different ways, on what it means to live a full and coherent life.

Creation

The significance of ourselves and our work depends on the value of creation, and the value of creation depends on its final destiny.

—Miroslav Volf, *Work in the Spirit*[7]

One of my favorite bedtime stories to read to my children—and to myself, for that matter—is *The Princess and the Goblin* by George MacDonald, a nineteenth-century Scottish clergyman, storyteller, and poet. It tells the tale of the young princess Irene, her lovely great-grandmother, and her friend Curdie, a miner boy, who ultimately rescues Irene from being captured by mine-dwelling goblins. The sequel to *The Princess and the Goblin* is called *The Princess and Curdie,* which tells of Curdie's own encounter and adventure in coming to better know Irene's great-grandmother, who serves as a winsome and beautiful Christ figure in both stories.

It's nearly impossible to capture the amazing way MacDonald draws out the nature of God through his depiction of this lovely mystical woman, ever changing her form and shape while at the same time deepening the constancy of her wisdom and kindness. She is old and young at the same time, simultaneously strong yet frail, far distant and immediately close all at once. She takes unexpected forms as a weaver of silk, an old beggar woman, a luminous beauty, a keeper of pigeons. Still, she is always recognizable to those who know her well and always a haunting mystery to those who do not.

Curdie is perplexed by her many dimensions and forms, and asks her to explain her true identity. Her reply: "Shapes are only dresses, Curdie, and dresses are only names. That which is inside is the same all the time." He questions, "But then how can all the shapes speak the truth?" She responds, "It would want thousands more to speak the truth, Curdie, and then they could not."[8]

For me, this short fairy-tale exchange tethers occupation and vocation together in a delightfully simple way, but it also illuminates something deep about the character of God. It is not incongruent for us to know him as Father and Mother, humble Servant and triumphant King, Lion, and Lamb. There is enough room in the fullness of God for him to be all and one simultaneously.

But the even more astounding truth is we are created to be just like him. Genesis 1:27 says, "So God created mankind is his own image, in the image of God he created them; male and female he created them." The vast dimensionality of God draws us to wonder first and foremost at God in all of his fullness. At the same time, it invites us to reimagine the full range of what it means to bear his image.

Like the princess's mysterious great-grandmother, we wear many "shapes and dresses" in any given day: running errands, filing a legal brief, cultivating a new friendship, filling out school forms, building a spreadsheet, and many others. Yet Irene's great-grandmother shows us these many "dresses" do not contradict each other; they are all part of the bigger truth, which is our whole self. Such a picture does not limit our identity. Instead it offers us tremendous freedom to explore the full range and complexity of our identity as image bearers.

I know full well God is infinitely manifested in ways I cannot be. Still, the great-grandmother's response to Curdie contextualizes the confusion I feel when it seems like I just have too many "dresses" to keep straight. It reminds me the complexity I feel in my personhood is not a problem to be solved or winnowed down into more manageable parts. Instead, the myriad dimensions of my occupations are a wonderful part of my identity as an image bearer of an infinitely dimensioned creator.

As a person—never mind as a woman—I find this to be profoundly good news. It is a mind-blowing, heart-exploding reality that Christ created us to be like him: to bear his image and love the things he loves.

Rooting our identity in God's creation as *imago Dei*, the image of God in the world, is a profoundly different identity than what culture offers us. Modern culture, for example, might encourage us to "find ourselves," but this proves more difficult than it seems since fewer than one in three Americans (30%) consider themselves to have a strong sense of their own personal strengths and weaknesses and even fewer (24%) say they have clear goals for where they want to be in five years. In contrast, Christianity invites us to trust that we are already fully known, mindfully crafted in great detail as Psalm 139:13 says: "You created my inmost being; you knit me together in my mother's womb."

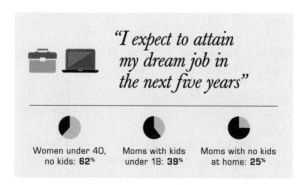

"I expect to attain my dream job in the next five years"

| Women under 40, no kids: **62%** | Moms with kids under 18: **39%** | Moms with no kids at home: **25%** |

Instead of having to prove our worth through endless striving, we can rest confidently, knowing our work and worth are inherently dignified from creation because we bear God's image. Furthermore, while Christ invites us to obedience that will stretch and refine us, he also promises the load will not crush us. Matthew 11:30 assures us his yoke will be easy, and his burden will be light. This contrasts with our cultural mantra of "do more, be more"—which demands we give all we have, whatever the cost. And that cost is high: 72% of women feel overstressed and more than half of all mothers (56%) feel overcommitted.

I gained insight into what it means to bear the image of God a few years ago when I was on a spiritual retreat in the Shenandoah Valley. In the morning, a spiritual director encouraged me to stop analyzing my spiritual life and instead to try to simply enjoy God. I have to confess I thought this sounded terrible. I had no idea where to begin.

I decided to begin by taking inventory of things I enjoy. I like reading. There, I had something. I like reading narrative or fiction. Better. I like Annie Dillard. Bingo. I grabbed her Pulitzer Prize–winning nature journal, *Pilgrim at Tinker Creek*, from the shelf in my cottage and set off into the cool February-frosted woods.

After hiking along the icy creek for a bit, I sat down on a bench and started reading. As I paused to wonder at Dillard's incredible power of description for things like circling hawks and clear blue skies, I sensed an impish question tap me on the shoulder: "So, you like words, do you? You like Annie Dillard's description of the

HOW DOES GOD FEEL ABOUT ME?

I know God is pleased with my choices — 40%

I'm not sure if God is pleased with my choices — 44%

I often worry God is not pleased with my choices — 16%

2/10 women have a very clear sense of what God wants them to do with their lives

water bug and the cosmos, eh?" I began to sense the Lord meeting me in my desire to meet him. "I happen to love words too," this welcome but admittedly weird impression-of-a-voice whispered in my conscience. "In fact, I like words so much, I am The Word."

Whoa. For the first time in my life, I began to get it: the love God has for his creation, for me, the way he created me to bear his likeness. In this shared passion for words, I began to see the connection between my work and his work. He invites me to embrace my love of words simply because he enjoys sharing them with me. He is curious to see what I might do with them. I finally understood he entrusts his wildly passionate love of words to a bumbling fool like me simply because that same wildly passionate love extends to me.

To know this is how God sees my gifts, my work, and my various responsibilities changes how tightly I hold on to them. It makes it easier to hold even my most strident efforts, hopes, and plans a little more loosely. It changes my perspective from needing to white-knuckle my way through life to "have it all" and instead encourages me to ask how I might steward all the various dimensions of my life more fully, more creatively, and with better imagination.

This simple encounter provided significant help to me, but this kind of help is rare. A full 44% of women admit they're not sure if God is pleased with their priorities and choices—an anxiety that is reflected by the eight in ten women who admit they don't have a very clear sense of what God wants them to do with their life. And while this number drops to 32% among practicing Christians, it still demonstrates the majority of people—even Christians—do not primarily think about their work and identity as mirroring God's work and identity in the world. And when women are asked what areas they most want to improve, their top two responses are personal development (20%) and commitment to church or religious activities (22%). For these women, the creation story offers good news: there is a meaningful way to connect faith and work.

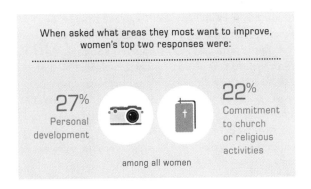

When asked what areas they most want to improve, women's top two responses were:

27% Personal development

22% Commitment to church or religious activities

among all women

At a birthday dinner party several years ago, I sat next to a theology and literature scholar who made an observation about Flannery O'Connor I will never forget. She said, "Writing is the means God gave her to experience his grace." I didn't understand it fully at the time. But, in the years since, I have come to think it is one of the most truthful and wonderful ways to think about my own work and diverse responsibilities. In whatever form they take, in every season of life, my relationships and responsibilities are ways God has given me to experience his grace. My work and the tensions of my work are an ongoing invitation into deeper knowledge of God and myself.

Constraint

The effective part of the will is not effort but consent.
— Simone Weil, *Paying Attention To The Sky*[9]

Earlier this year I needed to make time to go to New York City for a daylong lineup of meetings. We live four hours from the city, so I thought I would take the day, spend the night, and head back early the next day. But it turned out to be not quite so simple. My three little kids were tired and clearly wanted me home. My husband was tied up with international travel for work. Both our parents live out of state. And I couldn't ask just anyone to watch our kids overnight, since my six-year-old daughter has an autoimmune disease that requires special treatment that not many are sufficiently trained to administer.

If I had known how complicated it was going to be, I would have scrapped the whole plan and set up Skype calls or sent a colleague in my place. But it was too late for that now. And I felt stuck.

It's just logistics, but these are the moments when I begin to wonder if this whole calling business is simply too much. It is the kind of moment that tempts me to just quit my job, stop writing, hang it all up, and go get my toenails painted. It was a moment when I lost all confidence in my ability to make good decisions about my life and priorities, a feeling in which I am not alone. Less than one-third of mothers (30%) say they feel very confident they are making the "right" choices in their life right now, and that number is even lower among women who do not have children (24%).

But what was it about this particular decision that rattled me so much? It wasn't just the complexity of logistics. I sensed the undercurrent was weightier than that. I finally had to recognize my angst was rooted in a

DECISIONS, DECISIONS

"I am very confident I'm making the 'right choices' in my life right now"

24%
Women under 40, no kids

30%
Moms with kids under 18

33%
Moms, no kids at home

more pervasive challenge. This trip brought me toe-to-toe with *constraints*.

Constraint is not usually a pleasant word. It means boundaries, limitations, the feeling you get when you get your hopes up only to be told no. Formerly, I would have chosen freedom over constraint any day, but several years ago one little black dress showed me how beautiful constraint can really be.

In 2009, Sheena Matheiken conducted what she called "The Uniform Project" as an exercise in sustainable fashion. She would wear the same "little black dress" every day that year. But every day, she would also create a new look with donated, reused, handmade, or vintage accessories. The project was named in honor of children who wear a school uniform but find ways to make it their own with brightly colored tights, untucked shirts, rolled-up sleeves, hair accessories, and so on. And while the project sounds simple enough, the outfits she designs are incredible![10]

The Uniform Project helped me see that the tensions I face in my calling as a part-time working mother are not primarily a problem of culture, history, or economics as I assumed them to be. This little black dress helped me realize my fundamental tension was instead rooted in finitude—in being finite. Basically, I wanted to be able to do six things, and I could only accomplish two. I wanted to be present to my kids, available to my clients, engaged with my husband and friends, active at my church. But no matter how I tried, I could not figure out how to be in four places at once.

The significance of the Uniform Project—its use of constraint as a creative outlet—struck me deeply in 2009 when I first heard about it. Perhaps that was because our family was living in England at the time while my husband worked hard in full-time graduate school and I worked part-time and cared for two babies under age two. Constraints were what you might call my "bread-and-butter" in those days.

But this little black dress showed me how constraints can, in fact, be the source of tremendous freedom, clarity, and creativity. It offered me a new construct for making sense of my constraints. I realized the project was able to achieve something creative, meaningful, and fun only because it was always the same dress as the foundation of each outfit. In fact, it was the very constraint of a daily routine that made the whole project so unexpected and imaginative.

As I reflected on the counterintuitive effect of constraint in this fashion project, I started to see the benefit of limitation everywhere. In his own explanation of limitations, contemporary Japanese painter Makoto Fujimura writes, "An artist learns very early that creativity demands boundaries and limits to thrive."[11]

It's not just art and fashion. I began to see this principle of limits at work in ecology and agriculture, marketing and messaging, business and entrepreneurship, and countless other spheres of work. The discipline to stay tethered to one crop, one message, one product, one distinctive is proven practice. Honoring limitation has a curious way of yielding abundance.

It's easy to look at my own limitations in terms of time, energy, abilities, and finances, among others and see them as impediments to my calling. But the Uniform Project beckoned me to reconsider. The project's zany tights, patterned vests, and feathered headdresses asked me to reimagine my limitations — to see my constraints not as problems to be solved but as the *means* for creativity and focus in my life and work.

When I think of the years I spent as an overly ambitious twentysomething, I can now see how paralyzed I was by the sheer abundance of possible careers to pursue, relationships to engage, cities to live in, trips to take, degrees to acquire. Where my mind was once consumed by a never-ending calculus of hypothetical scenario-planning, my life now is tethered to actual, ordinary scenarios. I once reveled in the freedom of possibilities, but now that constraints are part of my daily life, I find more purpose and, unexpectedly, more freedom. I no longer entertain, for instance, a once-persistent suspicion I might be called to practice law because the exact number of times I have thought about prosecuting legal offenders when I am up with a baby at night is zero. Likewise, my once-strong interest in corporate communications fizzled when I realized reading the newspaper is a pretty low priority for me. That is not to say having children quelled my interests or ambitions. But it did — beneficially — narrow my focus.

Paradoxically, I found the new constraints of family life helped me see my true loves and unique responsibilities more clearly. For example, I often found myself falling asleep at night thinking about a friend's new project and how I could help. I found myself using evenings to write reams of text that will never see the light of day simply because I enjoyed doing it. I continued to find ways to connect people and ideas—a significant aspect of my vocation. These same skills had been present to some degree in my earlier professional life, but it was only through the context of constraints that they became focused, creative, efficient, and new.

Like the constraints of the little black dress, the limitations of my life helped me fashion a way forward I would not have otherwise.

Incarnation

> Christianity is inescapably down to earth and incarnational—I say "inescapably," as most of us, at one time or another, try to avoid an incarnational faith.
> —Kathleen Norris, *The Quotidian Mysteries*[12]

My trip to New York ended up working out after all. And here's why: When I was pregnant with my now two-year-old son, we had a wonderful part-time nanny named Annie. She broke our hearts a few months after my son was born when she decided to move to Poland to live with her grandmother for several months to learn more about her family history. We were happy she had the opportunity but sad to lose her.

We finally got back in touch around the time I was trying to schedule my trip. She was once again living in Washington, DC, and had been missing my kids.

She asked if she could see them or watch them some evening. Simultaneously, my husband had a meeting move from his company's European headquarters back to its New Jersey office. We decided to coordinate our trips and build in an overnight together in North Jersey while Annie and the kids enjoyed a little reunion. It ended up being fun, restful, and refreshing for all of us. It reminded me God always makes provision for the things he calls me to pursue. It reminded me his economy is infinite. It reminded me God understands my constraints but is undeterred by them.

In fact, one of the more radical claims of Christianity is that we worship a God who willingly took on constraints. We worship a God who bent low and took on flesh — who became incarnate for our sakes. He lived, suffered, and died as one of us. He was born into a particular historical moment, to particular parents, in a particular place, and in the midst of particular circumstances, just as we are. This central fact sets Christianity apart from any other faith on earth. And it has some pretty profound things to tell us about what God thinks of our so-called limitations — especially if you're like me and prefer to greet limitations with kicking and screaming or maybe a good, long pout.

In Luke 2 we see God taking great care to speak into the ordinary realities of human life, specifically the constraints of time, place, relationships, circumstances, and flesh.

Time: Christ was born into a specific historical and cultural moment, "while Quirinius was governor of Syria" (Luke 2:2). We too must take up our calling in time and season and within a particular cultural and political context.

Place: Christ's earthly family had a certain geographic identity just as we do, which is why Scripture is careful to let us know, "Joseph also went up from the town of Nazareth in Galilee to Judea, to Bethlehem" (Luke 2:4). Our own neighborhoods, cities, and places matter to God and to us.

Relationships: Jesus' familial ties and identity are marked as significant by their elaborate description. After a tour of the family tree, the text tells us Joseph "belonged to the house and line of David. He went there to register with Mary, who was pledged to be married to him and was expecting a child" (Luke 2:4–5). Families and relationships place certain context and limitations on our life and identity.

Circumstances: Events that seem beyond our control are events God can still use for his purposes. God's own Son was born in a stable "because there was no guest room available for them" (Luke 2:7). A political census, limited finances, and poor timing were all constraints that gave rise to Mary's trough-side delivery.

Flesh: God was born to a woman, as we all are: "While they were there, the time came for the baby to be born, and she gave birth to her firstborn, a son. She wrapped him in cloths and placed him in a manger" (Luke 2:6–7). By his ordinary birth, Christ affirms the confines of our bodies and the myriad ways they limit us with physical weariness, sickness, infertility, and aging.

These particular confines draw our attention to the fact that God himself, who has all the universe at his disposal, was not all atwitter about maximizing potential, "having it all," or chasing down effectiveness. Of course, his power was not constrained, as we see in his miracles and resurrection. But he chose to take on human constraints. With all his wisdom, he did not choose to transcend time or space or decades or even the rote mechanics of gestation, labor, and delivery. Rather, he chose to work through the same ordinary human constraints we all face—he did not see these as impediments but rather as the purpose.

There is something deep in the incarnation for understanding our own calling in the midst of constraints. At creation, God spoke humans into being and dignified them by allowing men and women to bear the multi-faceted dimensions of his image in their flesh. At the incarnation, God once again bent low in kindness but dignified us this time by taking the frailty, feebleness, and finitude of our mortal image upon himself.

A few years ago I met a new friend who is now one of my best. She is a successful filmmaker and had just had her first baby. When I asked how she was doing, I was surprised to hear her reply: "Kind of terrible, actually." This stark honesty made me love her immediately.

She told me about a film project she had been working on as a consultant. It was a project she cared about deeply from the beginning, and one she hoped to help produce by raising a substantial part of its necessary funding. At a critical juncture in the project, all doors that had been open to her for funding on other projects remained stubbornly shut, and she was worn out. She had been enduring a high-risk pregnancy at the time and was wary about what motherhood might require of her over the same months when the film was being released. She was also helping her husband plant his new church and felt significant responsibilities to that calling. Despite her longing to say yes to the project, after several months of toiling to make it work, she decided the constraints of her life were instead leading her to say no. The night before she saw me she learned this film had just been accepted to the Sundance Film Festival. And, as she told me that day, "When I found out, I just wept."

This type of story is where our constraints stop being inspiring and start to get ugly. These kinds of limitations are not to be taken lightly. And these are the moments we have to believe the incarnation really does have something good to tell us about limitations or else we will lose our minds and maybe even our faith.

Giving my daughter five shots a day, for example, is more than just an inconvenience. It's a heavy weight. My sister's severely limited diet and low energy do not have a quick or easy fix. Caring for ailing parents, navigating the single life when you'd rather be married, battling infertility, working two jobs to keep your kids clothed, and countless other constraints weigh women down every day. These are the constraints we rail against. And they're not just disappointing; they are wounding. We begin to wonder if such wounds will handicap us from flourishing for the rest of our lives.

These are moments when the incarnation pushes us beyond Christmas to Easter. At Christmas, we see God come as a baby, quietly dignifying our most simple, ordinary limitations. But on Good Friday, Jesus takes on the fullness of our finitude in death. Still, Easter reminds us — even at the height of human limitations on the cross — that God does not perceive them as we do. God is not surprised by even the ultimate constraint of death, nor is he deterred by it. Instead, through Christ's resurrection he draws each of us into the heart of the mystery that is the Christian faith: "The one who believes in me will live, even though they die" (John 11:25). Or, interpreted into my own daily life and experience, "Though I am limited, yet may I find abundance."

When we reflect on our constraints through the life, death, and resurrection of Christ, we can begin to make sense of the constraints that introduce tension into our own lives. On one hand, we can look for the practical ways constraints bring clarity and creativity to our life like we see in the Uniform Project. At the same time, it means looking for ways God might be using our feeble limitations to bring resurrection where our constraints truly feel beyond hope. Isaiah 53:5 summarizes the great mystery of Christianity when it says, "He was pierced for our transgressions, he was crushed for our iniquities; the punishment that brought us peace was on him, and by his wounds we are healed." To the extent we bear God's image and look to Christ as the model for our own life, we must be willing believe — as God healed the world through Jesus' wounds — it is also through our own wounds he can heal the world.

Cormac McCarthy captures this heartbreakingly beautiful truth in *The Road* when he writes, "All things of grace and beauty such that one holds them to one's heart have a common provenance in pain. Their birth in dust and ashes."[13]

Covenant and Community

Persons cannot be whole alone.
—Wendell Berry, *The Body and the Earth*[14]

Part of the grief and ash in my own life comes from spending my childhood, for many reasons, bouncing between several different schools, churches, neighborhoods, families, and homes. I often joke these frequent changes taught me a lot about adaptability and flexibility—both skills that have served me well in my life as a working mom. But the truer, harder reality is that I came into adulthood with very little sense of identity or belonging.

In college, for example, I remember envying friends who owned bags full of worn-out T-shirts they'd gotten running a 5K with their dad, or being a camp counselor, or playing tennis at a local racquet club. Not because the T-shirts themselves were all that great, but simply because they gave testimony to a life lived in community. Even now, when I am washing or folding a stack of my own kids' cheesy T-shirts from our annual church picnic, a winter basketball clinic, or winning the coloring contest at Ledo's pizza, I periodically feel a hint of redemption. Our family belongs here. We know our people. We have our place.

Sadly, for many women today, this communal identity is a crucial, missing piece of their lives. Less than half of all women (42%) strongly agree they are connected to a strong support network of family and friends (and this number, at 29%, is even lower among men). This not only means the majority of women lack practical community support, such as having others to help by watching kids, running errands, or cooking a meal. It also means women are navigating complex choices and priorities without the relational support of others. Proverbs 15:22 warns us against this: "Plans fail for lack of counsel, but with many advisers they succeed."

But even more fundamentally, this widespread communal poverty is problematic because it mars our identity as image bearers of God. From creation we know we reflect the image of a triune God who, by his very nature, is community. Genesis 1:26 is explicit in this: "Then God said, 'Let us make mankind in our image, in our likeness.'" God is not one, but three-in-one as the creeds teach us. As such, God is not an autonomous individual in the way we conceive of modern individualism. And Scripture assures us, neither are we.

We are thoroughly relational, communal beings. It is hardwired into us. What *imago Dei* claims so radically, in fact, is that we become more truly ourselves only as we increasingly give ourselves to God and others. Dr. Curt Thompson, a psychiatrist who authored the book *Anatomy of the Soul*, studies this relational hardwiring as it is revealed in neurobiology. He observes that even from our smallest infancy, our brains grow and develop properly only in response to neurobiological cues and exchanges with other brains—other people.[15]

God gives us this image most clearly in the covenant of marriage. And, indeed, among married women, more than three-quarters (75%) say their marriage is their most common source of strong emotional support. Not only that, but a majority of Americans who are married say their marriage helps them to refine their understanding of priorities (56%), set better boundaries (51%), feel satisfied with their lives (57%), and become the best version of themselves (53%).

For centuries the church has passed down a three-fold understanding of

75% of married women say their marriage is their strongest bond of emotional support

MY MARRIAGE HELPS ME ...

57%
Be satisfied with my life

56%
Understand my priorities

53%
Be the best person I can be

51%
Set good boundaries

49%
Live out my purpose

33%
Connect to a community

HOW WOULD YOU DESCRIBE YOUR MARRIAGE?

70%
My spouse supports me

56%
It's fulfilling

51%
It makes me very happy

49%
God is important to my marriage

34%
It takes a lot of work

22%
I wish it were better

4%
I'm not sure if it will last

Christian marriage to help us understand its purposes: to be unifying, sanctifying, and life-giving. These fundamental dimensions of marriage also reflect Christ's relationship to his church (see Ephesians 5:25), and they speak broadly to all our relationships. Pressing into this framework of unity, sanctity, and fruitfulness honors the covenantal character of our relationship with every place and person to whom God has called us to meaningfully belong.

The purpose of my friendship with Susan, for example, easily matches against all three. Over the years, our friendship has taken on a richly covenantal shade of purpose, identity and belonging. We've encouraged one another in our work, attended the birth of one another's children, enjoyed time together with our husbands over dinner. In this way my friendship with Susan is unifying and strengthening in the myriad ways it provides companionship, constancy, and support.

Likewise, it is sanctifying. Just as my husband and I are constantly being refined as we bump up against each other day after day, sustaining a deep and close friendship inevitably means we hurt each other. We must regularly give and receive grace precisely so we can be made more holy and so we can better bear the image of Christ in our lives.

Finally, while the sexual union of marriage provides unique life-giving potential, in truth the point of every Christian life is to bear fruit. The "pro-creative" call of marriage is not simply about baby-making so much as it is evidence our relationships—even our most intimate relationships—are not designed to be insular or self-serving. The closer we are drawn into relationship, the more responsible we are to bear fruit and life outside ourselves for the sake of God's kingdom.

A covenantal framework for thinking about friendship, marriage, and community is especially important in our modern culture in part because we have so many tools and tactics for appearing as though we have relationships that, in truth, are not very sustaining. For example, while the vast majority of women in general (85%) and nearly the same number of moms (87%) say they have at least one friend with whom they can talk to about anything, approximately one-third (35% of women, 31% of moms) also agree they often *feel* lonely.

Women ranked friendship lower than any other priority

except religious involvement in how they spend their time—both vital components to community life. Only 14% say friendships are an important area to improve. This lack of priority may be why fewer than one in three Americans (27%) say they are extremely satisfied with their friendships, but it may also be a significant factor to explain why women often feel so polarized and isolated from one another.

There are practical explanations for friendship's low priority among women. Friendships will rarely take the place of family as a primary source of emotional support or weekly time investment, but friendships are a vital form of community. It is important to make time to develop and sustain them in spite of busy lives and busy schedules.

Still, to suggest this covenantal framework only pertains to personal relationships is to miss a key aspect of how community informs our identity, calling, and work. Community is as much about place as it is about people. Of the identity crisis that plagues modern life, Wendell Berry writes, "The lost identity would find itself by recognizing physical landmarks, by connecting itself responsibly to practical circumstances, it would learn to stay put in the place in which preference or history or accident has brought it; it would, in short, find itself by finding its work."[16]

For most of us, "finding our work" in the way Berry means is not simply to take a Strengths Finder test or reexamine a Myers-Briggs profile, though both are helpful and commendable tools. Instead, what Berry suggests is that we will find our work in the truest, most

Factors of
FRIENDSHIP

While very few women would rank friendship as their number one priority, it is still a significant factor in how they see themselves and how they navigate life.

FRIENDBOOK

update status

"I have at least one friend I can talk to about anything" — **85% of women**

"My close friends often provide emotional support in my life" — **84% of women**

"I am connected to a strong support network of friends and family" — **42% of women**

"Friendship is central to my identity" — **35% of women**

"I am extremely satisfied with my friendships" — **29% of women**

"Friendship is my first priority" — **6% of women**

More than 1/3 of women say they often feel lonely

fulfilling sense only within the context of community. That is, only by hemming ourselves in to practical realities and common life and relationships will we rightly be able to take up our full work.

For my husband and me, choosing to live in close proximity to our church, our office, close friends, and our kids' school, for example, is one way we try to acknowledge community is not just about people, but also place. By pursuing the work we each care about, we belong to certain needs and issues. We open ourselves to the ways work exposes our weaknesses and pride. And we trust that God works through our ordinary acts of faith to bear fruit now and in the world to come. As Gerard Manley Hopkins writes, "To lift up the hands in prayer gives God glory, but a man with a dung fork in his hand, a woman with a slop pail, give Him glory, too. God is so great that all things give Him glory if you mean that they should."[17]

Coherence

The only thing we really know about who we are is what we do.

—Marilynne Robinson, *When I Was a Child I Read Books* [18]

Last fall a friend handed me a dog-eared copy of *Kristin Lavransdatter* by Sigrid Undset, saying, "I think this is the most true book I have ever read." With such a fervent recommendation, I picked it up right away. The book is a 1920s Nobel Prize–winning trilogy about a young girl coming of age in thirteenth-century Norway. Despite its setting in time, as I became increasingly engrossed in the narrative, I found myself wholeheartedly agreeing with my friend's assessment.

Near the end of the book, Kristin is on pilgrimage to join a convent for the final season of her life. As she walks, she contemplates her life, meditating on all the turbulent ups and downs of a complicated marriage, faith, and family. As she begins to feel the full form and weight of her life's blessings, griefs, and terrible mistakes, she reflects:

> Surely she had never asked God for anything except that he let her have her will. And every time she had been granted what she asked for—for the most part. Now here she sat with a contrite heart—not because she had sinned against God, but because she was unhappy she had been allowed to follow her will to the road's end. [19]

For me, this sober realization captures what is at stake for women as they consider how to best order their commitments in our modern age. Like Kristin, women need little help imagining all they might want for themselves over the course of a life: children, a fulfilling career, a loving spouse, a beautiful home, or perhaps something entirely different. At the same time, both men and women long to know they are choosing well. Each wants to believe the pursuit of their longings and desires will lead to flourishing. It is important to note here the fundamental questions we face as women about our sense of purpose and fulfillment are not so much "woman questions" as they are human questions. None of us wants to spend our final days feeling contrite and foolish. We all want to know we did our best to steward life well.

Yet the challenge for women today is the growing reality that stewarding life well often means sustaining several different roles and responsibilities at the same time. As one study reveals, an average mother in 1965 spent only eight hours a week on paid work, whereas that number almost tripled to twenty-one hours a week for mothers in 2011.[20] At the same time, a recent Pew Center study shows women as the primary breadwinner in four in ten American households, demonstrating a significant socioeconomic shift in how women are being asked to prioritize their time.[21]

That said, overall, mothers are generally able to spend the most time in the realm of their biggest priorities. For example, while more than eight in ten mothers (83%) say family is their top priority, seven in ten (69%) also say family is the top consumer of their time. However, work is the one notable exception. While only 1% of mothers say working is a top priority for them, almost a quarter (23%) say it is a top consumer of their time in a normal week. This trend is mirrored among women without children. Only one in ten say career is their top priority, but almost half (45%) say it is the top consumer of their time. And women without children have time and priority misalignment in other areas as well. For example, more than half (57%) say family relationships are their top priority, but less than a quarter (23%) say family is also where they spend the most time.

Clearly, this increasing responsibility to be working, and possibly being the primary breadwinner, is a point of tension for many women. And this is when the national dialogue of the work-family balance begins to reach fever pitch. However, our challenge is not primarily one of

PRIORITIES VS. TIME

#1 Priority	#1 Time Commitment
Family	Career
Personal development	Family
Church	Personal development
Career	Friends
Friends	Church

Women under 40 with no kids

#1 Priority	#1 Time Commitment
Family	Family
Personal development	Career
Church	Personal development
Friends	Church
Career	Friends

Moms with kids at home

#1 Priority	#1 Time Commitment
Family	Family
Church	Career
Personal development	Personal development
Friends	Friends
Career	Church

Moms with no kids at home

balance. In the midst of our most priority-stretched, off-kilter days, what each of us really needs is the assurance that life makes sense. That it holds together. That it can be whole.

It's not so much about finding balance as it is about *coherence. Coherence* is a word that evokes seamlessness rather than categories, wholeness rather than perfection, a life shaped by discernment, complexity, and constraints rather than a clean-cut pie chart. For me, this word is especially important because I feel the tug and disparity between my roles and responsibilities *all the time*. I need a framework that is big enough and honest enough to account for not only the quantity of my responsibilities but the distinctive quality inherent to each one and still, somehow, hold them all together in a way that makes sense. Such a framework encompasses my finitude and constraints.

A few years ago I was working in a reduced part-time role with a small arts investment group I helped to start. I had scaled back my time considerably to be at home with our daughter and for the birth of our son, who is eighteen months younger than she is. I had recruited my good friend Laurel, a fellow freelance mom with kids, to do the graphic design layout for an upcoming investor conference brochure. And, in what is predictable form for us, we were pushing right up against a print deadline. Our daughters were both still toddlers at the time, so we decided to meet at her house and crank out the final details together.

We set up camp with our MacBooks at her kitchen table, brewed some coffee, sent the girls to the basement to play, and prayed our baby boys would sleep for a good, long stretch. It was a memorable day of many different roles converging — nursing mother, professional, and friend. When Laurel's husband came home from work a few hours early to take over kid-duty for the afternoon so we could finish up, he walked in on both of us sitting side by side at the table, each typing one-handed with a baby on the breast and the girls coloring across from us. As he jokingly remarked, "On so many levels, this would never happen at my office."

I offer this example not as a window into how to juggle or somehow "have it all," because in truth when I remember that day I can still palpably feel the stress of it. I do not morally recommend this work/home/life setup, but for us, in a situation of limited options, we managed.

There was nothing particularly "right" or "better" about our decision to parent and push hard to finish a deadline simultaneously. Other mothers may have handled the scenario differently, and it would have been just as fine for them. And that is the beauty of coherence. The exact mechanics of how we hold our lives together is not the point. The point is that we attempt to hold them together at all.

Coherence, apart from balance, is unique in this regard. Balance has a way of homogenizing the diverse and distinct nature of human work, too often allowing the conversation about tension and complexity to devolve into a conversation about plans and logistics, strategies for more efficient living. Coherence allows me to hold together things that, in fact, do not abide together naturally. It allows for the possibility that the work of delivering, nursing, and raising a child can be wholly distinct from the work of speaking, managing, and writing—and a life that is coherent enough to encapsulate both. Under the umbrella of coherence these dissimilar passions and efforts can all coexist peaceably and sensibly alongside one another.

And coherence even allows, so long as my work and identity are rooted in Christ, that my efforts may be radically unbalanced and off-kilter at various points along the way. Under coherence I do not have to cordon off "life" as being somehow separate from "work" or vice versa when the "life" part starts to feel a lot like the "work" part. Instead, it allows each aspect of my responsibility and effort, role and desire to flourish according to its distinct and diverse nature.

Consent

> The effective part of our will is not effort, but consent.
>
> —Simone Weil[22]

This simple, truthful observation dropkicks us right back into the heart of the gospel. We consent to our interests and longings as a way to image God and show forth his beauty, creativity, and kindness. We consent to our constraints trusting he will use them as he did at the incarnation to bring forth abundance. We consent to community as a reflection of the Trinity and God's covenantal relationship to his people. We consent to allow God to use our lives as he will, trusting that as we yield and avail ourselves, he will lead us through confusion and constraint into rich coherence. Kathleen Norris writes,

> The Christian religion asks us to place our trust not in ideas, and certainly not in ideologies, but in a God who was vulnerable enough to become human and die, and who desires to be present to us in our everyday circumstances. And because we are human, it is in the realm of the daily and the mundane that we must find our way to God.[23]

So much of the conversation about the role and struggles of women today reflects the increasing opportunity women have to steward their gifts and abilities faithfully in a number of areas of life. Conversations about "having it all" and "leaning in" and "work-life balance" are good reminders to be thankful for the abundance we enjoy. At the same time, the church has important things to share with both men and women about limitations, brokenness, and disappointment — to offer the rich hope of Christ and his kingdom to women who are feeling lonely and stressed and stretched beyond capacity. ◆

WONDER WOMEN

Navigating the Challenges of Motherhood, Career, and Identity

RE/FRAME

BY ANDY CROUCH

There are two kinds of mornings in our home.

On the good mornings, all four of us have rested well and wake early. Our kids, Timothy and Amy, make their own lunches, brush their teeth, and head cheerfully out the door to school, several minutes early. My wife, Catherine, and I each exercise and pray, then she packs up her laptop and textbooks and—this is where our family becomes a tiny bit odd—heads off to teach quantum mechanics to a roomful of bright and motivated college students. I start my day relaxed and grateful, ready to write, sing, edit, and speak.

There are a few good mornings like this in any given month.

The bad mornings? Everyone wakes up too late and too crabby. Our adolescents revert to grade-school levels of sloth and distractedness, colliding in the hallway on the way to the shower. Both ask Catherine (always Catherine, never me) to pack their lunches two minutes before they leave. At least one misses the bus. A tense negotiation follows about which parent has more time to drive. Students turned in their lab reports to Catherine at 1:00 a.m. and questions are piling up in her inbox; I have missed four different deadlines in the past twenty-four hours. The screech of the wheels pulling out of the driveway is the sound of a whole day starting at full tilt, everyone already stressed out and no time to pray.

And that's not counting the mornings—about one hundred in a given year—when my calling has taken me by plane or train to somewhere far away. I have no idea how Catherine survives those mornings.

Here is what I do know.

I know Catherine is called to the world of labs, whiteboards, office hours, lasers, and journals—all the tools of her calling as a professor of physics. She is called there because human beings, image bearers of the creator God, are called to join the Creator in his joyful attention to the world he has made, declaring it "very good" and unfolding every aspect of its very-goodness. She is called there because she showed up to our first real conversation, at Café Algiers in Harvard Square, carrying a pile of physics papers she both comprehended and delighted in. She is called there because at every step of her formation as a scientist, others—fellow students, mentors and teachers, friends and counselors—have affirmed, encouraged, and celebrated her vocation.

I also know Catherine is called to the world of carpools, music lessons, packing lunches, emailing teachers and guidance counselors, and making dentist appointments—all the duties and rituals of parenthood. She is called there because human beings, image bearers of the creator God, are most fully themselves when they give themselves to the flourishing of others, fruitfully multiplying the human family and tending to its youngest and eldest members. She is called there because in that first real conversation at Café Algiers, we discovered to our mutual surprise that each of us was quite sure our primary calling in life, should we find a spouse, was to have children. She is called there because others surrounded us at our wedding a year later, and prayed, in the appropriately provisional words of the Book of Common Prayer, "Bestow on them, if it is your will, the gift and heritage of children, and the grace to bring them up to know you, to love you and to serve you," and because, two times, after months of waiting and hours of travail, that gift was given.

I know these two callings are just the beginning—that Catherine is also called to friendship, to serving our neighbors, to teaching and counseling and praying with others in our church family, to making music and preparing feasts and tutoring and being longsuffering and compassionate. She is, by the greatest grace of God in my life, called to be a helper "suitable" to me (Genesis 2:18), one who can quench my aloneness and willful loneliness, constrain me to become like Christ, and know and hold me until we are parted by death. And she is, most deeply and truly, called to follow Jesus, called to imitate him in her living and trust him in her dying, to be lifted up by his hand on the other side of eternity and given a white stone with the true name only she will know.

This is what I also know.

I know every step of Catherine's career as a physics professor has been unconventional at best and confounding at worst—intermittently attentive advisors, recalcitrant equipment, ambiguous results, and ungrateful students. On the best days, her tremendous gifts of synthesis and explanation lead to abundance in the lab and the classroom; on the worst days, the same preparation and talent seem to sink and vanish like rain on a cracked desert plain.

I know there is nothing that can call forth a deeper sense of inadequacy than accompanying our two children through childhood and adolescence — that nothing else brings such paralyzing frustration alongside pure delight. Some days their need for us seems to far exceed our ability to respond; some days our yearning for them meets only distracted inattention. Our children are unpredictable bundles of need and independence, pouring out thoughts and emotion and retreating into silence, with little regard for the scheduled family times on our seven shared Google Calendars.

I know most everything has gone better for us than we ever could have imagined and that nearly every facet of our lives has been more difficult than we expected. I know our sandals have not worn out and our feet feel constantly weary. I know we have been blessed with the greatest of friends and have felt impossibly alone. I also know these clay jars have held a treasure, that in these afflictions there has been unexpected comfort, and that more often than we deserve, we are overtaken with something you could only call an eternal weight of glory.

But there is something I don't know: how all this is supposed to fit together. Not just how to fit together Catherine's (and my) many callings, which seems like putting together a single jigsaw puzzle from several different boxes, but the deeper question: how do joy and suffering cohere, the glory and the mundane cohere, and unexpected success and persistent frustration cohere?

I suppose what I really would want to add to Kate Harris's marvelous exploration of vocation, creation, constraint, incarnation, community, and coherence is just this sense of knowing and unknowing.

There is so much we can know about what and who we are called to do and be, and there is so much we cannot know. This would be true even if we were entirely different in our callings and choices. It would be true if Catherine (like so many senior female scientists) had never married and never borne children, free to single-mindedly pursue her career. It would be true if she (like so many devoted Christian women) had set aside career to single-heartedly raise her children. All the perplexity, all the gratitude, all the loss, all the joy would still be there. Differently apportioned perhaps, but still there. No system, no matter how nuanced and careful; no plans, no matter how strategic and flexible; no faith, no matter how informed or prayerful—nothing can "solve" the "problem" of career, family, and calling.

For career, family, and calling are not problems to be solved. They are mysteries, and in the end they are minor mysteries. They pale beside the real mystery, which is how our lives are held in a greater life, how our death shall be overcome by a greater death, and how even the smallest things in our days—the lunch boxes, lab reports, and logistics—can become doorways to the life that really is life.

"Therefore, my beloved" — my beloved
Catherine! — "be steadfast, immovable, always
excelling in the work of the Lord, because you know
that in the Lord your labor is not in vain"
(1 Corinthians 15:58 NRSV). ◆

....

Andy Crouch is executive editor of *Christianity Today*
magazine and author of *Playing God* and *Culture Making*. He
is a senior fellow of the International Justice Mission's IJM
Institute and a member of the Board of Advisors for the John
Templeton Foundation.

AFTER YOU READ

....

- Which word resonated most with you as you read: *vocation, constraint, community,* or *coherence*? Why do you think that word stood out to you?

- If you apply this more holistic idea of "vocation" as something that encompasses all of who you are, what are words or ideas you might use to describe your vocation?

- How have you seen yourself live into those passions — into your vocation — outside of just your career? How has your role as a mother and wife formed your vocation? How have your hobbies or personal interests informed your sense of vocation?

- Name some of the constraints in your life. How might you begin to see those constraints as gifts instead of hindrances? How could they be your "black dress"?

- Why is it so crucial to pursue a sense of vocation within community? How has your community shaped you and informed your sense of calling? How can you seek more support in that?

- Jesus was born into a certain time and place and context — and so were you. What is it about your specific time, place, and social context that you think you were "made for"? In other words, what gifts of yours are best designed for our day and age, as well as the community you live in?

- What are two or three practical steps you could take to more fully embrace your vocation in the different spaces of your life—at work, at home, in your community?

SHARE THIS FRAME

Who else needs to know about this trend?
Here are some tools to engage with others.

SHARE THE BOOK

- Any one of your friends can sample a FRAME for FREE.
  Visit zondervan.com/ShareFrames to learn how.

- Know a ministry, church, or small group that would benefit
  from reading this FRAME? Contact your favorite bookseller, or
  visit Zondervan.com/buyframes for bulk purchasing information.

SHARE THE VIDEOS

- See videos for all 9 FRAMES on barnaframes.com and use
  the share links to post them on your social networks and share
  them with friends.

SHARE ON FACEBOOK

- Like facebook.com/barnaframes and be the first to see new
  videos, discounts, and updates from the Barna FRAMES team.

SHARE ON TWITTER

- Start following @barnaframes and stay current with the
  trends that are influencing and changing our culture.

- Join the conversation and include #barnaframes whenever
  you post a FRAMES related idea or culture-shaping trend.

SHARE ON INSTAGRAM

- Follow instagram.com/barnaframes for sharable visual
  posts and infographics that will keep you in the know.

Barna Group

ABOUT THE RESEARCH

FRAMES started with the idea that people need simple, clear ideas to live more meaningful lives in the midst of increasingly complex times. To help make sense of culture, each FRAME includes major public opinion studies conducted by Barna Group.

If you're into the details, the research behind the *Wonder Women* FRAME included one thousand surveys conducted among a representative sample of adults over the age of eighteen living in the United States. The survey was conducted from June 25, 2013, through July 1, 2013. The sampling error is plus or minus 3 percentage points, at the 95% confidence level.

If you're really into the research details, find more at www.barnaframes.com.

ABOUT BARNA GROUP

In its thirty-year history, Barna Group has conducted more than one million interviews over the course of hundreds of studies and has become a go-to source for insights about faith and culture. Currently led by David Kinnaman, Barna Group's vision is to provide people with credible knowledge and clear thinking, enabling them to navigate a complex and changing culture. The company was started by George and Nancy Barna in 1984.

Barna Group has worked with thousands of businesses, nonprofit organizations, and churches across the country, including many Protestant and Catholic congregations and denominations. Some of its clients have included the American Bible Society, CARE, Compassion, Easter Seals, Habitat for Humanity, NBC Universal, the Salvation Army, Walden Media, the ONE Campaign, SONY, Thrivent, US AID, and World Vision.

The firm's studies are frequently used in sermons and talks. And its public opinion research is often quoted in major media outlets, such as *CNN, USA Today*, the *Wall Street Journal*, Fox News, *Chicago Tribune*, the *Huffington Post,* the *New York Times*, *Dallas Morning News*, and the *Los Angeles Times*.

Learn more about Barna Group at www.barna.org.

THANKS

Even small books take enormous effort.

First, thanks go to Kate Harris for her excellent work on this FRAME—combining her insights and experience with all that research and producing what we pray is a prophetic, nuanced, yet practical book for women in the twenty-first century.

We are also incredibly grateful for Andy Crouch's beautiful and personal reflection on the daily realities of navigating vocation, parenting, and identity within a marriage.

Next, Barna Group gratefully acknowledges the efforts of the team at HarperCollins Christian Publishing, especially Chip Brown and Melinda Bouma, for catching the vision from the get-go. Others at HarperCollins who have made huge contributions include Jennifer Keller, Kate Mulvaney, Mark Sheeres, and Shari Vanden Berg.

The FRAMES team at Barna Group consists of Elaina Buffon, Bill Denzel, Traci Hochmuth, Pam Jacob, Clint Jenkin, Robert Jewe, David Kinnaman, Jill Kinnaman, Elaine Klautzsch, Stephanie Smith, and Roxanne Stone. Bill and Stephanie consistently made magic out of thin air. Clint and Traci brought the research to life—along with thoughtful analysis from Ken Chitwood. And

Roxanne deserves massive credit as a shaping force on FRAMES. Amy Duty did heroic work on FRAMES designs, from cover to infographics.

Finally, others who have had a huge role in bringing FRAMES to life include Brad Abare, Justin Bell, Jean Bloom, Patrick Dodd, Grant England, Esther Fedorkevich, Josh Franer, Jane Haradine, Aly Hawkins, Kelly Hughes, Steve McBeth, Geof Morin, Jesse Oxford, Beth Shagene, and Santino Stoner.

Many thanks!

NOTES

1. Lillian Calles Barger, *Eve's Revenge: Women and a Spirituality of the Body* (Grand Rapids: Brazos Press, 2003), 118.

2. Anne-Marie Slaughter, "Why Women Still Can't Have It All," *The Atlantic*, June 13, 2012, http://www.theatlantic.com/magazine/archive/2012/07/why-women-still-cant-have-it-all/309020/.

3. Sheryl Sandberg, *Lean In: Women, Work, and the Will to Lead* (New York: Knopf, 2013).

4. "Tim Gunn," http://en.wikipedia.org/wiki/Tim_Gunn.

5. Andi Ashworth, *Real Love for Real Life* (Colorado Springs, CO: Shaw Books, 2002), 73.

6. Annie Dillard, *The Writing Life* (New York: Harper Perennial, 1989), 21.

7. Miroslav Volf, *Work in the Spirit: Towards a Theology of Work* (New York: Oxford University Press, 1991), 93.

8. George MacDonald, *The Princess and Curdie* (West Valley City, UT: Waking Lion Press, 2006), 38.

9. Simone Weil, "Paying Attention To The Sky" in *Waiting for God* (New York: Harper Perennial, 1951), 143.

10. Sheena Matheiken, "The Uniform Project Picture Book," *The Uniform Project*, May 2010, http://theuniformproject.com.

11. Makoto Fujimura, "Jefferson's Bible and the Tears of Christ," *The Biologos Forum: Science and Faith in Dialogue*, March 31, 2012, http://biologos.org/blog/jeffersons-bible-and-the-tears-of-christ.

12. Kathleen Norris, *The Quotidian Mysteries* (Mahwah, NJ: Paulist Press, 1998), 77–78.

13. Cormac McCarthy, *The Road* (New York: Knopf, 2006), 118.

14. Wendell Berry, "The Body and the Earth" in *The Art of the Commonplace* (Berkeley, CA: Counterpoint, 2002), 99.

15. Curt Thompson, *Anatomy of the Soul: Surprising Connections between Neuroscience and Spiritual Practices that Can Transform Your Life and Relationships* (Carol Stream, IL: Tyndale Momentum, 2010).

16. Berry, "The Body and the Earth," 106.

17. In an address he gave on St. Ignatius of Loyola's writings on "The Spiritual Exercises."

18. Mailynne Robinson, *When I was a Child I Read Books* (London: Picador, 2013, reprint edition), 34.

19. Sigrid Undset, *Kristin Lavransdatter*, trans. Tiina Nunnally (New York: Penguin Classics, 2005), 1071.

20. Kim Parker and Wendy Wang, "Modern Parenthood: Roles of Moms and Dads Converge as They Balance Work and Family," Pew Research Social and Demographic Trends, March 14, 2013, http://www.pewsocialtrends.org/2013/03/14/modern-parenthood -roles-of-moms-and-dads-converge-as-they-balance-work-and -family/.

21. Wendy Wang, Kim Parker, and Paul Taylor, "Breadwinner Moms," Pew Research Center, May 29, 2013, http://www.pew socialtrends.org/2013/05/29/breadwinner-moms/.

22. Weil, "Paying Attention To The Sky," 143.

23. Norris, *The Quotidian Mysteries*, 77–78.

Share Your Thoughts

With the Author: Your comments will be forwarded to the author when you send them to *zauthor@zondervan.com*.

With Zondervan: Submit your review of this book by writing to *zreview@zondervan.com*.

Free Online Resources at
www.zondervan.com

Daily Bible Verses and Devotions: Enrich your life with daily Bible verses or devotions that help you start every morning focused on God. Visit www.zondervan.com/newsletters.

Free Email Publications: Sign up for newsletters on Christian living, academic resources, church ministry, fiction, children's resources, and more. Visit www.zondervan.com/newsletters.

Zondervan Bible Search: Find and compare Bible passages in a variety of translations at www.zondervanbiblesearch.com.

Other Benefits: Register to receive online benefits like coupons and special offers, or to participate in research.